Come Fly with Me

Tales from a Master Falconer

A pen-and-ink drawing I did as a gift for my friend, Juanice Christian, who assisted me with the typing of my manuscript.

Come Fly with Me

Tales from a Master Falconer

Mark Joseph Good
"The Owl Whisperer"

Florida

Paperback: 979-8-9907566-1-8
E-book: 979-8-9907566-2-5
Hardcover: 979-8-9907566-0-1

Cover Design and Page Layout by Nancy Koucky, NRK Designs
Edited by Karin Nicely
Illustrations by Mark Joseph Good
Photos by Mark Joseph Good and Ethan Marcus Good
(unless otherwise noted)

Printed in the United States of America

Florida

*Dedicated to all those who have supported
my efforts and programs over the years.*

Contents

Preface

The following is a collection of true stories about the experiences of the author, Mark Joseph Good, as a master falconer.

Some of these tales are connected, while others took place at different times during Mark's career working with raptors, spanning a thirty-year time period or longer, excluding childhood memories, of course, which were obviously much further back in his life.

Mark attempts to show the reader the spiritual side of working closely with these fascinating creatures. He offers direction for those interested in possibly becoming a falconer but also addresses some alternate possibilities for others who are intrigued by raptors but do not have the time, land, or money to fully pursue falconry.

With a record of great success, Mark has also used his birds to aid in his work to help troubled youth, those struggling with addiction, and habitual offenders.

Through his words, Mark strives to enlighten readers about his deep emotional connections with his birds.

Introduction

Throughout my lifetime of some sixty-five years, I have repeatedly been told by many people—friends, family, even perfect strangers recently met—that I should write a book. They all seemed to somehow see the same things in me, and they asked for more. To them all, I say, "Thank you for believing I have something to share." Maybe I do. Read on. I hope they were right and that maybe you, too, will agree.

Special Mention

My friend and mentor, Jerry, passed away from heart complications in a hospice facility back in Cherokee, North Carolina. Earlier, after suffering a heart attack, Jerry lost his beautiful bondmate, Copper. After being released from the hospital, he was feeding her when she attempted to kill a domestic dog. She sensed his weakness, was too strong to control, and flew away. I believe I saw her once in the Florida National Cemetery while visiting my father there. She lost Jerry and Jerry lost her, but the life they shared together was one of dreams.

Jerry was a teacher. He was a Master Eagle Falconer. He served in the United States Navy as a pilot. He was Native American. Jerry even played professional football for the New Orleans Saints. He was a unique individual. It has been five years since his passing, and I miss him.

He died in hospice on my birthday, and I trust he is flying somewhere with the eagles that he loved so much. Godspeed, my friend. Thank you for the life you taught me. I owe so much of it to you. Thanks again, my old friend.

My personal version of a praying mantis,
specifically drawn for this book.

The Praying Mantis

"Praying mantids can grab and bite hard—especially the big ones! Be careful as they might not let go if they grab a finger.
As a child, my babies did make me bleed now and again."

Initially, when I hear "praying mantis," I still think of martial arts and certain poses or defense moves. But for the purpose of this chapter, I am in fact writing about the actual insects that get quite large. They are perfect little six-inch predators found in almost every garden, almost everywhere.

Why the praying mantis, you ask? Simple enough, I suppose. They intrigued me as a child. Even growing up in the city lifestyle of Baltimore, Maryland, I could find them and their egg cases attached to the bushes around the neighborhood. Other kids would find them, too, and bring them to me as pets of sorts. My dad had a small city garden, and I'd put them there until it got cold. Then, I'd bring them inside, where they would winter on my mother's fake indoor plants. No kidding! My mother was a real trooper each day I went off to school. My charges needed to be fed and watered while I was out. Imagine feeding those giant insects raw ground beef from a tablespoon! Not to mention drinking water, too. But Mom did it—every day! Thank you, Mom.

I didn't know it then, but those winged creatures were amazingly aggressive killers. They kept insects away that would damage plants, but they had another talent, too: killing small birds! This surprised me a great deal, but it was also my introduction to understanding our "circle of life" and how predators fit in. As a boy, I had no idea how these insects would one day set me on course to the similar predator connection offered in the art of falconry. Back then, I had no idea what falconry was.

Birds and Pirates

I love birds!

I always have, and I always will. As a child, it started with my godparents owning a little budgie. They lived next door, so I saw the little fellow every day. I thought he was cool because he was allowed to curse. I'd ask why *he* was allowed but *I* was not. My dad was a deacon in the church, so I think you can figure it out. I didn't really understand it then, but I did what I was told. I also admired any good pirates in movies depicting the days of the swashbucklers, but most of all, I loved the colorful parrots perched on their shoulders. "Polly want a cracker?" still rings in my ears. As a child, my parents gave me a fake plastic one that sat attached to my shoulder. Captain Sparrow would have been proud.

The living birds entered my life as time moved forward. Quaker Parrots, a Lovebird, an Indian Ringneck, Conures, a Blue-and-gold Macaw, and a Sulphur-crested Cockatoo taught me how to prepare for the other species over time.

My future birds would become very interesting, to say the least, but that was yet to come. In the late 1970s, I would move to Colorado, coming home to a place I'd never been before. I loved it! I was lucky to secure a job in private forest management as a forestry technician in Black Forest, Colorado—almost heaven. It was there that I met my first living raptor up close, a large female Great Horned Owl, as she killed a rat in the snow. The encounter changed me somehow. I wanted more.

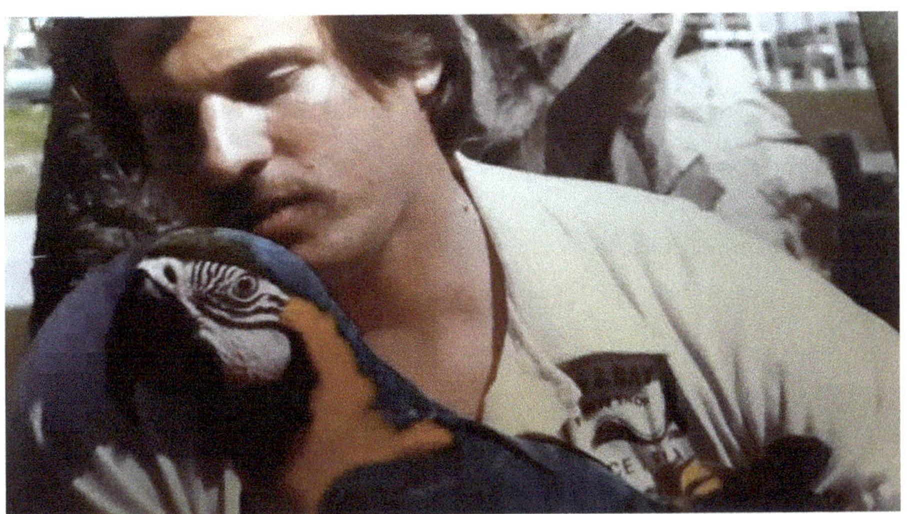

This is Casey. I rescued her from a pet store that had her locked in a shoebox in a dark closet. I could hear her screaming.

Robert Cook, Sr., pictured with my wife, Coleen, in 1979 at The Cave of the Winds, Colorado Springs, Colorado. We had permission to explore (with a guide) sections of the caverns not open to the public.

Robert Cook, Sr.

"Try to experience new things. Keep your life interesting.
Don't be shy. Learn to dance or sing, if you can.
Embrace life; it is far too short."

Someone else I met was Mr. Bob Cook from Nebraska. He even knew Johnny Carson from his hometown. Mr. Cook became a millionaire twice in his life but lost it both times. Sadly, he trusted an unscrupulous business partner. But he instilled some advice in my heart that has guided me well in everything I have done, including falconry. His words of advice were: "Mark, you are young and talented. You have the world by the seat of its pants and don't even know it. My advice to you: As you go through life, you will note things that catch your attention. Maybe hang gliders, race cars—who knows? Do yourself a favor with everything that you see; make an honest effort to experience it yourself at least once. Skydiving? Try it! If you manage to actively do ten percent of these desires, you will have lived a life worth sharing."

I have lived my life by these words, and I am comfortable with my achievements. I applied it to everything in my life, including falconry. I became a forest ranger and more: a wildland firefighter; a certified prescribed fire manager; a forestry supervisor; a SCUBA divemaster; a cave diver; a shipwreck diver; a drug addiction counselor; a vocational instructor for the county school board; and more. And yes, a falconer, currently master level. I served thirty-one years with the State of Florida.

Cherokee Jerry

"My friend Jerry died on my birthday.
He went home to Cherokee, North Carolina,
and then went home to fly with the eagles that he loved so much.
He is missed."

ate one evening, working as a ranger assigned to a campground, I was performing my first raptor-related campfire program. For the event, I had borrowed a screech owl from a local wildlife rehabber, but my knowledge was very limited. Likewise, my lack of handling skills at the time. There were over one hundred people in attendance. At the end of the program, I noticed one fellow didn't leave with the others. He wanted to speak with me. So, we did.

His name was Jerry Hollifield, but he was known to many as Cherokee Jerry. He was proud of his Cherokee heritage and of growing up on Cherokee lands. He had taught wildlife behavior at a college in North Carolina, and he was a master falconer, specifically a Golden Eagle master falconer—the only one in the country at the time. His Golden Eagle was a female named Copper that Jerry had hand-raised from a chick. She weighed fourteen pounds and carried an eight-foot wingspan. We clocked her, one day, with a radar gun in a dive at 180 miles per hour! Jerry used her to hunt deer, antelope, turkey, and anything else she desired, including foxes and coyotes. That beautiful lady was a skilled hunter.

Copper was trained to hunt from horseback, on draft horses, which Jerry rode bareback. True story. (This is where the little budgie with the foul mouth would say, "I shit you not!") Jerry would first bring Copper from the mews then bring the horse out, mount, and call Copper to him. She would be on Jerry's arm as he rode.

One thing led to another, and I was hooked, especially with the big raptors.

Jerry offered to train me, to be my sponsor, to take me on as his apprentice falconer, as he had done for many others before me. It would take seven years minimum and lots of work to become a master falconer. It was going to be a ride!

So, I trained and studied and finally took my exam with the government, passing with an 83% the first time. I'm kind of proud of that. *Let the games begin!*

An advertisement for Masters of the Wind, the program Jerry and I created for Cypress Gardens (photo credit: Cypress Gardens)

Apprentice Falconer

"So, you think that you want to be a falconer. What are your reasons?
Discuss it with yourself."

When someone starts out in falconry, there are federal and state rules and regulations to follow, including stipulations about what type of bird you can keep and train, usually a Red-tailed Hawk, a great bird for hunting rabbit or squirrel. I was fortunate to have Jerry, an eagle falconer, as a sponsor. He also owned a Harris' Hawk.[1] I got Duster, my Red-tail, as my first falconry bird, but I worked a lot with the big eagle named Copper, which was very cool, indeed. She was a dinosaur!

Duster taught me about hawking. Mostly rabbits were taken, but I learned much about raptor behavior with that bird. And yes, we bonded. We learned to read one another's body language. Sadly, on our first day of hunting, a storm blew in and I lost him. It broke my heart. But not being a quitter, I took off work for five days to search for my Duster. On the fifth day, over two miles from where I'd lost him, I located my boy on a power pole. I called him to my glove. He responded and went home with me after he had a good meal. Jerry was amazed! So was I. Duster was my partner for over two years of successful falconry before being set free in Florida.

---

1   (American Ornithological Society, 2023) While every effort has been made to correctly present bird names according to the American Ornithological Society, the form of "Harris' Hawk" was used in this text rather than the AOS spelling, "Harris's Hawk," because the former is used more widely in falconry circles.

*Wind Dancer, a Red-tailed Hawk I trained for Anheuser-Busch
at Cypress Gardens, is shown "mantled" over a kill,
which means the wings are spread to hide the food from enemies.*

Red-tailed Hawk Duster

Apprentice Adventures

If falconry is done correctly, your bird(s) will bond with you. So, exactly what does that mean? Many new falconers will speak of bonding or having bonded with their bird(s) and yet they have not. Bonding is not trained tolerance. You can make a bird fly to you for food even if it doesn't like you. But that isn't falconry; that's ego, sadly. It's a show that I avoid.

Bonding is trust. It's a partnership, an understanding that you are now partners, bonded in a life-and-death struggle in which all raptors live, especially in the wild on their own. Being a partner with a falconer should greatly extend a bird's life. My Harris' Hawk, Terra, who lived to thirty-three years of age, was one of the top ten oldest registered Harris' Hawks in all of North America. She is sorely missed, my "Lady Hawk."

With Harris' Hawk Terra on the hunt.
Note the terrain—jungle hawking!

I learned during our adventures that raptors do not kill for sport like a cat does. They kill for food, to survive. The sport part of falconry is something that man created, and it is not all of the falconry population. I fly and hunt for my birds. It is a spiritual activity, sharing the trust developed out in the wild. My birds know that they eat what they kill. I take nothing from them. This trust created a partnership that will last a lifetime. I have left my bird in the woods, in the wild overnight, and returned the next day to retrieve them before returning home. Trust: it is critical for working with a raptor.

One morning, my Red-tailed Hawk, Duster, and I went rabbit hunting on a huge piece of property, acreage as far as you could see. They say that a raptor, on average, can see an object the size of a baseball in color up to a mile away! (Budgie screams, "Bull crap!"—but it's true!) Duster proved it that day. The nearest wood line from where I stood with Duster was well over a mile away, some 5,280 feet and more. Yet Duster saw something move from so far away. I released him, and he flew straight off in the direction of his interest. I jumped into my four-by-four SUV, in chase, with the hopes of a front-row seat to the adventure.

Some minutes later, I caught up to him, finding him perched high in a pine tree, yet something was different there. He frantically continued calling me. Upon investigation, I found, hidden in the brush, a cardboard box with five puppies in it, maybe six weeks old, but one was already dead. Assumingly to relieve some of their guilt for abandoning the young animals, the human individual had left two open cans of dog food at the scene. Amazing. Thank you, Duster. He watched as I loaded the puppies into my SUV and drove immediately to our veterinarian. We saved the remaining four dogs, each getting a home by day's end. One was named Duster in the hawk's honor for a very special job well done. These birds do think, and they do have personality and very good memory. Don't let anyone tell you otherwise.

Personal Protection

"Beautiful but deadly, a raptor can hurt you. Trust takes time. Always use caution in everything you do with your bird."

One surefire way to be sure your bird is bonding with you is how he/she reacts to others around you. Are strangers accepted without hesitation, or does your bondmate show the desire to protect you from them?

My Harris' Hawk, Terra, would defend me aggressively. If someone approached from behind, she was my eyes and personal alarm as she screamed her warnings. I learned to be very careful with her as physical contact did happen between her and certain trespassers. The days of me letting observers watch her freely came to a cautious end.

I have maintained other raptors with the same mentality regarding protecting their handler. It requires much caution and preparation when taking birds into public places. After all, raptors are not puppies or kittens. They are serious apex predators. Most of our human population has no idea of the capabilities of an adult raptor. So, we teach.

The Matador

"Dancing Hawk"

When one starts down the falconry path, the average apprentice is emotionally overloaded with the things that are yet to come. There is simply so much to learn, and experiences will differ from person to person based on the chosen raptor species and the geography in which they live. Even in these United States, hunting in Montana is a dramatically different experience than hunting in, say, Georgia.

A falconer needs to learn the lands in which he plans to fly his raptor. One also needs to use great caution in releasing your bird into the territory of a larger raptor that could possibly be a species enemy. Raptors will kill other raptors. Use great care to protect your partner. She depends on you.

Other things—feral dogs, for example—can be an issue. Barbed-wire fences also kill raptors. And I will fly nowhere near a major roadway, if possible. A fellow falconer friend's two beautiful Harris' Hawks, flying in a cast (a pair) when the rabbits crossed a major highway, gave chase and were both hit by an eighteen-wheeler. Yes, both were killed. Gun hunters will shoot at your birds, too, which is why I quit hunting in Wildlife Management Areas. It seems everything wants to kill your bird. You must protect them.

Surprisingly, raptors have trouble surviving in a human world. They say that only a small percentage, maybe two out of every ten, of them survive to sexual maturity. Poisons, shootings, barbed wire, storms, automobiles, other raptors, larger predators, and…rabbits.

Rabbits, you say?! Yes, rabbits! I laugh when I hear folks express pity for the hunted rabbit and curse the hawk as a killer. Are you personally a meat eater? Enjoy fast-food burgers, maybe? Well, it's no different with raptors. They need to survive.

They eat meat—nothing else.

So, please don't fret when you think of raptors being removed from the wild for falconry. They should live longer and be healthier because of it.

Some years ago, my sponsor, Jerry, had a very large female Red-tailed Hawk. She was a big girl. Jerry "entered her in" (falconry term) on large game. In fact, he was used to hunting the largest game in the United States that you could hunt with a bird. Not surprisingly, he felt rabbits provided little challenge.

However, Jerry had trained several falconers for the Medieval Times Entertainment franchise, and one of them convinced him to hunt jackrabbits in the Arizona desert. It would be during a camping trip with fellow falconers. *It should be fun*, he thought. So, at daybreak, the group went hunting for Mr. Bunny, and it wasn't long until a very large Jack decided to make a move. Then it was on!

Jerry's girl was what we call sharp-set, which means in perfect hunting weight, in solid health, and ready to conquer the world. Sharp-set birds are totally alert. She wouldn't miss a trick.

The action was hot and heavy, with neither combatant willing to give up in their life-and-death struggle. It is, after all, how they exist.

After a ten-minute on-and-off chase between the two, Mr. Bunny started to show signs of exhaustion. That was where the hawk should shine. Gliding in chase gives hawks time to rest, so this behavior alerted the falconer group to be ready for action. *It won't be long now*, they thought.

The rabbit made a break for an area of thick vegetation, likely in hopes of hiding. The hawk was hot on his trail! The distance was closing rapidly, and the audience cheered like they were at a professional sports exhibition.

Feet and talons extending, the hawk was poised for the kill when, in the blink of an eye, Mr. Bunny flipped over in mid-jump, kicking the hawk in the head and knocking her out cold! *What?!*

Never underestimate the little guy.

Being out in the middle of nowhere meant no veterinary care of any kind was available. Jerry sadly held his bondmate, fearing the worst as the potential outcome. Sometime in the early morning hours, she passed away in his arms. I know that terrible feeling well. It breaks your heart. Again, I urge you to never underestimate a rabbit. They are tough critters.

Knowing this story oh so well, I took my Red-tailed Hawk rabbit hunting anyway. The bird would be Duster. Now, Duster was a wild-caught hawk raised by his parents. We were not bonded, per se, but we were still a very functional team. A friend told me about a city lot, maybe four acres or so, surrounded by man and developed. I hated the location but loved the field. Wildlife was trapped there, and rabbits bred with nowhere to go. They were overpopulated. We could thin things out a bit. So, off we went.

I briefly mentioned that Duster was parent-raised for a reason. They fed him snakes and taught him how to hunt them. He'd chase small mammals, but he loved reptiles. I could tell on our hunts by his "flight body language" if he was targeting a snake. He would hover over it before attacking. During his time with me, he was 100% accurate, foolproof in his attacks.

In Florida, we have six species of snakes that are venomous. Duster knew how to approach them from overhead, but he would not attempt a direct kill. He would land in front of them, and the dance would begin. Spreading his wings, he'd begin a hypnotic sway, making the snake watch the wings for a strike. Duster would try to make the snake strike at a wing, which is mostly feathers. A snake-strike hitting feathers does nothing, and the bird can then "foot" the target before it knows what is happening. Duster was a skilled matador, loving this type of confrontation. The bad part is the chance of it being a venomous encounter. The falconer cannot assist due to the risk of either the bird or themselves getting bitten. This is when your heart pounds out of control as you watch and pray for your bird's well-being. I have even wrestled the snake away from Duster to prevent the reptile's death. This is also dangerous, and a trade for bagged meat is the only option that the birds will tolerate. Trust is of the utmost importance.

Some folks are truly afraid of snakes. Instead of actual photos,
I decided to just draw the scene.

Old-School Falconry
vs. a New World

What I have noticed most in my thirty-plus years of falconry is the way people have tried to force change on the sport. In my humble opinion, it isn't necessary to change something just for the sake of change. I believe the old saying is something like, "If it ain't broke, don't try to fix it." But it seems to be human nature to do just that.

I trained under an old-school falconer. It only makes sense that I became one, too. Following many techniques of Mongolian hunters who work with giant eagles to hunt wolves, Jerry passed on their secrets in raptor training and care. They literally live with their birds. Their bonds are very strong, and their lifestyle is admired by falconers worldwide.

When Jerry and I traveled west to the Rockies to witness various raptors maintained by Western falconers, I noticed the changes happening before my very eyes. I had heard a great deal about a particular Gyr Falcon. The Gyr is usually mostly white, but it also has darker phases, and some look almost black. The bird we met was a white one—a beautiful raptor indeed!

We were scheduled to go out with this awesome bird the following morning. The air felt electric! I had never seen a Gyr in the flesh. We were going with the Gyr's owner to do some pheasant hunting for Ring-necks.

When I noticed an electronic tracking device on the kitchen table, however, I looked at Jerry with a question on my lips, and he motioned for me to hold my tongue. Remember that Jerry was an old-school falconer and an old soul, as it were. I could tell he had made a mental note of it, too. The falconer/owner started to brag a bit about how much money the system cost him. These things do not impress me. I maintained my polite mode and just listened.

For the record, if you are a falconer who conforms to the use of modern electronics, feel free to enjoy yourself. I mean no disrespect, but I prefer old-school methods, such as bells on the ankles for tracking. We joke that our birds sound like Santa Claus is on his way!

I watched the man attach a transmitter with a long wire to the bird's tail. To me, this just looked plain stupid. But I was there to learn. He then removed a rather large hand-held control box complete with everything needed to pilot a drone (or so it seemed to me). Jerry's eyes continued to tell me to keep quiet.

Okay, then. Testing, testing. *Beep, beep, beep.* He released the bird, and off she went like a bat out of hell, flying at speeds only a falcon can achieve. Yes, off she went!

Wait a minute, I thought. *Isn't the bird supposed to be partnered with the falconer so that they can work together?* It didn't look that way. I watched the beautiful Gyr fly due north until she disappeared from sight. Gone!

I looked at the falconer and asked, "Do you still have her transmitter?" I didn't hear the beep any longer. The answer was no. *Oh, wow*, I thought. *This isn't good.*

We jumped in our trucks to give chase, bypassing all of the game fields, and still no beeps. The receiver remained silent.

The handler mentioned a large water tower several miles to the north where pigeons would roost. Maybe she went that far?

Eventually, we saw the tower appearing up ahead. The receiver started to beep, slowly at first but then faster. She was in the area.

We parked at the base of the tower, and there were pigeons everywhere. After a few minutes, we spotted the Gyr chasing one of them. She sure could fly!

But to me, this was not falconry. We used up the entire day in chase, and it would be dark in an hour. How was the owner going to call his bird home when it was surrounded by flying food? There were over 100 pigeons! His electronics became useless, and his bird simply ignored him. We were partners to no chase. No excitement. No thrill. No partnership. What a disappointment.

I was wondering if he was going to leave her there overnight and return in the morning when I saw her stoop (dive) on a target that she "punched" with clenched fists, knocking the bird to the ground. She then attacked it to make her final killing strike by breaking the bird's neck with that special falcon notch on the beak used just for that purpose.

The falconer quickly retrieved her as fast as he could. To each his own. I'll stick to my old-school training, thank you.

The Odd Things We Learn

"Freefall"

In addition to my many duties with the forestry service, I managed their 2,600-acre dirt-bike park in Florida—motorcycles, trails, and wildlife sharing the same space. Amazing! One day, a young boy and his mother flagged me down, needing assistance. It seems that they had located a baby owl, helpless on the forest floor, which had fallen from the nest. I was surprised everyone was careful around the little bird. It could have been easily run over. Evaluating the scene, I located the parent birds. Barred Owls. Their hooting reminds me of monkeys in the jungle. Mom and Dad were high in the canopy of large oak trees some fifty feet up. They, too, were helpless. I named the little guy Freefall so we could call him something besides "the baby owl." So, how would we return him to the adult owls?

Enter my friend Mary from a local rehabilitation center. Her advice and instructions were priceless! Mary advised me to find some nylon rope and a plastic milk crate, and we happened to have both items in one of our trucks. Several of us located the nest tree and tossed a line to its highest point. Securing the line, we created a tripod effect to balance the box, which became our nest. Insert Freefall. We then hoisted the nest box high into the tree. 100% success! We checked on the birds daily, and Freefall fledged, growing into an adult owl.

Raptors can be unbelievable parents, willing to defend their young to the death. Knowing that makes me understand that the Barred Owlet's parents knew we were trying to help their offspring. I feel privileged when a wild animal allows me the opportunity for these hands-on encounters.

Years ago, as a park ranger, I conducted nighttime Owl Prowls—nature walks in the dark of the woods. We allowed no flashlights except for those used by me and other staff members, and only for emergencies. Full moon evenings were

Lofting little Freefall to his new home is his milk-crate nest

the best. One other item made my nature walks different from most: I took a live owl with me, tethered to a glove. This always got the attention of native wildlife. Usually, that was a good thing, but not all of the time.

One evening's scheduled Owl Prowl proved to be one of those exceptions. That night, ten campers, one armed officer, and I embarked on a dark, moonlit excursion into the wild. I was blessed with the company of a young Great Horned Owl that I had adopted (legally) earlier that year. Her name is Shiloh. I still have her thirty-two years later! (More on her in another chapter.) As we walked, Shiloh would hoot that wonderful song that only a Great Horned Owl can do. And yes, she got the attention of other residents of the forest. What a wonderful, clear, moonlit night with perfect temperatures and not a cloud in the night sky. I happily thought to myself, *And I get paid to do this?*

I started to turn and face my guests for a head count and *WHAM!* Something crashed into my face, hitting me squarely between the eyes! It hurt, and I felt blood running down my face. Wow! But Shiloh seemingly remained calm and stayed on the glove, mildly irritated. This surprised me because it turned out I was attacked by an owl. My second in line had a front-row seat, as it were. The identification: a female Eastern Screech Owl, red phase. Well, holy crap! I should have thought it through better, but February is breeding season for the southern-east-coast birds, and when were we walking? Yep, you guessed it: right after January and before March. You get the picture. Momma Owl did not want us near her nest. So, we moved on.

For the record, I was smiling ear to ear. With almost all raptors, the sex can be determined by size. The female is usually one-third larger than her mate. This is why most falconers prefer flying a hen. A bigger, tougher bird catches bigger game. Jerry's female eagle, for example, commonly took 160-pound prey! It still amazes me to this day.

To All the Birds
I've Loved Before

"Bonding with an Owl"

Working with raptors professionally offers the opportunity to meet and handle many different species of birds. Legal ownership (stewardship) allows you to get close and to possibly bond with one of these predators. For me, knowing other falconers helped, too. Jerry and I once drove over two thousand miles to meet and hunt with a Goshawk in the Rocky Mountains. His name was Doctor Death. And yes, he lived up to his name.

My first falconry hawk was Duster, the Red-tail mentioned in chapter five. My second falconry hawk, a Harris', was my lady hawk, Terra. And owls started finding their way to my front door much like the praying mantis population had when I was a boy. Word was spreading of my efforts.

I met the Great Horned Owl Shiloh in 1991. She had eaten a rat that had consumed rat poison. It had almost killed her, and the poison had caused her to lose 99% of her vision. The day I met her at a rehabilitation center, she was in a large flight pen with other owls. The owner advised me, rather coyly, that I could take her only if I could load her into a carrier—on my own.

Hmmm, I thought. *I love a good challenge.*

I entered the enclosure carefully and slowly. With all eyes of lethal predators on only me, the door lock clicked behind me.

I focused on the female owl perched in front of me. This was a large first-year bird, and she had been through hell and back, including months of recovery. As she just stared at me, I felt like she was looking into my soul. It was almost spiritual in some strange way. So, I balanced the carrier on the perch and opened the door after first introducing myself.

This was my very first owl whisper.
It was a wild bird, after all. I appeared calm, but I was not.

"Darlin', I'm Mark, and I'm here to offer you a new life if you want it. But we need to prove to this nice lady that I'm the right guy for the job." In a whisper, I added, "She doesn't think I'm up for it." (This was my first official "owl whisper." Later, I came to be known as The Owl Whisperer.)

Well, that big girl understood and marched straight into the box! No joke! I was in owl heaven. Onlookers were shocked. I tried to act like it was no big deal, but inside, I was exploding with joy. To this day, we are still bondmates. A lifetime together and still counting the years.

We then took in a Barred Owl from a wildlife park in Crystal River, Florida. I named him Barnabas after the old *Dark Shadows* vampire character. I thought it fit. Several Screech Owls also found their way to our permits.

Then word spread to Virginia and a facility there with a Barn Owl no one could train. He was to be euthanized unless I could assist. I agreed to help. The bird was flown from Virginia to Florida with a very kind volunteer who delivered him to my front door.

"If it doesn't work out, I'll come back and get him," the volunteer assured me.

"Wow—thank you. But it *will* work out."

And it did. The Barn Owl became Gizmo. I still get Christmas cards from that volunteer. It has been some thirty years.

I once received a call from a veterinarian friend that a local school had a baby owl that kids had wrapped up in a shirt. They hid it from the teachers and almost killed it. I took him in, and we named him Gentry, and he grew into a beautiful bird, a Barred Owl. He passed away in 2022 on Christmas Day at the age of twenty-two years—old age for that kind of owl. I miss him.

Jerry and I contracted our services to Anheuser-Busch and founded Masters of the Wind, an educational facility within Cypress Gardens to teach children about raptors. School field trips were held there, and I worked with many species at the facility: Bald Eagles, vultures, falcons, Merlins, kestrels, Cooper's Hawks, kites, Great Horned Owls, Barred Owls, Barn Owls, Screech Owls, Red-shouldered Hawks, Red-tailed Hawks, and Crested Caracara, to name but a few. My experiences were growing and becoming well-known locally.

Over the years, there have been many birds I've handled through wildlife rehabilitation centers, too, getting hands-on experience to learn the medical aspects of raptor care. One never knows when a raptor emergency could leave you feeling foolish. I try to be prepared for any possible threat to my flock.

One bird I saved for the last in this chapter is a very special raptor indeed. His name is Thorin after the character in the Hobbit series of Oakenshield fame. He is a beautiful Eurasian Eagle Owl, my favorite raptor. The first time I saw one in real life was at a raptor program at an animal park in Florida—Weeki Wachee, the place with the mermaids. The bird was huge, and I was hooked.

It would be over twenty-five years until that species would enter my life again.

Nine years ago, I received a telephone call from a stranger in the western United States. He represented an owl-breeding facility. It appeared that a friend of mine, knowing my love for Eagle Owls, had contacted the facility on my behalf, inquiring about the cost, etc., involved in Eagle Owl ownership. They checked me out and were impressed with their findings. It seems they had a baby owl, and he needed someone like me to adopt him. They wanted to gift him to me. I was shocked.

Supposedly, all I needed to do was pay for his transit across the country, the cost of which would be somewhere in the $500 range. I called my wife with the story, and she felt we couldn't afford him. He was only thirty-five days old and needed to begin imprinting on me before thirty-eight days of age, the cutoff date for imprinting success. Retail chick costs at that time were as high as $5,000. At first, I said no—a serious thank you, but no. I didn't even have a building, called a *mew* in falconry, to house him in. Because of the federal codes and standards mews must meet, they are very costly to build. However, when I sadly went home that evening and stopped by my mailbox, I found a letter from the Commissioner of Agriculture saying my fellow employees voted that I was doing something right, so there was a check for $750. (Budgie says, "What?!") I took it to my wife, feeling closer to the little bird already. We decided to call the man back and accept. Thorin arrived at midnight on a Friday via United Air Freight. Within three days, he had finally arrived—at thirty-eight days of age. Imprint time.

After a two-hour drive home with Thorin, my son, the friend who'd contacted the breeder, and his son, we settled in for a long night of getting to know the little owl. I fenced off my living room with dog-kennel fencing, placed him in the middle, and then crawled inside with him. We immediately connected. I spent the night there, pretending I was a parent owl, feeding him mice. Consider how a raptor feeds their young: mouth to mouth. Appearances are crucial with this type of thing. In no time, Thorin was bonding with me; it was obvious.

On his first night in Florida,
Thorin and I spent the night together in this pen.

Of course, we still needed a mew. A structure for an owl that size would measure some fourteen to sixteen square feet with eight-foot ceilings. That meant lots of work and materials. Thorin would live inside until he could fly, which added to our bonding. I took off work for a week to make the best use of that time.

Not far from my home is a log-cabin company. They build with cypress logs. I dropped by, asking about scrap logs. When they heard the story, they agreed to donate everything needed to create Thorin's new home. I was in shock. Everything about that situation told me we were meant to be bondmates.

Much like during a barn-raising project, friends arrived to lend a hand. Very soon, the mew was ready, and Thorin moved in straight away. I stayed outside with him in the evenings until I sensed his comfort level had reached a certain point then left him on his own to explore his home.

Thorin's Tale of Intrigue

*"There is nothing good that can come from the
illegal wildlife trade and smuggling.
"If you suspect it, report it.
Too many animals die horrible deaths in the pet trade.
It sickens me."*

Thorin has a rather unique history, one that movies are made of, complete with crime, intrigue, and mystery. You might ask yourself, "Are we talking about the life of an owl?!" Yes, we are.

Some years back, a falconer decided to illegally make some money smuggling wildlife into the United States. His idea was to hire children in other countries to steal living raptor eggs from the species that nest on the ground, such as the Eurasian Eagle Owl. The children would take the live eggs to women in their villages to decorate the eggs as Easter eggs. Thus, fancy baskets fully decorated with absolutely no incubation became the death of many unborn birds. But our government's game wardens were watching. So, when a shipment of "Austrian Easter baskets" landed in San Francisco, they were waiting.

Sadly, only three eggs—black market value at $2,000 each—survived the trip. The eggs were carefully taken into federal custody and protection. They were distributed to three secret locations in the United States where they could be hatched and monitored. This was much like a witness protection program: the birds were evidence, and it could take years to prosecute the guilty parties.

One of those three hatchlings would be named Bomber. Bomber eventually was introduced to a large female Eagle Owl, and they fell in love and started their own family. Thorin was born to them some nine years ago at the time of this writing. What an unexpected turn of events.

In the previous chapter, I discussed how, within a month, little Thorin came to live with me. These first nine years together have been a real treat. He is a very special owl, and I am honored to be his keeper.

Otulissa Owl
and Strange Behaviors

I came home from work one day and went out back to check on my birds as usual. Stopping to visit my Barred Owl, Gentry, I noted a call from another Barred Owl *very* nearby, as in directly over my head, no more than ten feet up.

I looked into the tree, and there she sat—a large female Barred Owl! I spoke to her in owl talk, and she responded immediately with great enthusiasm. Admittedly, I thought this was unusual, but not terribly. I visit with many wild raptors throughout the area. She stayed all day and was active through the evening, being quite vocal with Gentry. She became a regular part of our property, and I named her Otulissa. She visited for years on a regular basis, and it was somehow comforting to me knowing that she was there.

Drop zone! Use caution under an owl like this!
She was close enough to touch her.

During part of the timeframe during which she visited us, I witnessed many interesting owl behaviors, but one really stood out.

My doctor at the time changed one of my prescription medications rather abruptly. The new schedule would have me waking up at 5:00 a.m. to swallow a pill! *I think not.* My wife told me to just set the alarm and live with it … more or less. Being stubborn, I decided against it. Such is life.

That evening, it was cool with a nice breeze. I opened the windows to enjoy the perfect sleeping conditions and was out cold before my head hit the pillow. Seemingly, minutes passed, but in fact, it had been hours when I was awoken by an extremely loud version of "Hooo, Hooo, Hooo … Who cooks for you?!" (the standard Barred Owl call).

I sat straight up in bed, trying to focus my vision as I became aware of my surroundings. What the heck?! I searched the room for an owl—not a terribly crazy thought at my house—but nothing was there. Was I dreaming? I looked at the red lights on the digital clock: 5:00 a.m.

"Hooo, Hooo, Hooo … Who cooks for you?!"

I love my owls, but this was loud, and I almost came out of my skin. But now I could focus on the sound and location of my organic alarm clock. Who would believe it?

Much like my first unexpected encounter with this unique visitor, there she was again; Otulissa sat on my windowsill, staring into my bedroom, waking me up at 5:00 a.m. to take my new prescription. Unexpected behavior, but oh so cool.

My version of a Barred Owl in pen and ink: Otulissa, a very unique raptor

The Swamp Owl

Late one evening at a local state-park raptor presentation, I learned firsthand about some of the time-honored spiritual beliefs Native American cultures hold regarding owls.

It seems that whoever organized the weekend events had hired us to bring in our raptors and had also invited a group of people from the Seminole Tribe of Florida to perform a cultural dance. However, when the Seminole group learned that I traveled with real owls, they refused to perform. I learned that people of many Native American cultures fear owls. To make things worse, a park staff member thought it was a joke to attach an owl feather to the tent entrance flap of the Seminole guests. How stupid and disrespectful could someone be? The tribal members were understandably alarmed and angered. They departed immediately, leaving all of their gear behind. I later learned that they blamed me as the perpetrator, thinking that I had retaliated because of their refusal to perform. Definitely not my style.

I asked my sponsor, Jerry, what his opinion was on the subject. After all, he was a member of the Cherokee Nation. I respected his tolerance with me, as his apprentice, gravitating toward owls. I like them; Jerry did not. He explained to me that historically, many Native Americans fear them. "They are signs of death," he said. "They represent darkness and evil … the supernatural."

While Jerry was personally less concerned about the birds' negative connotations, and some Native Americans revere owls, many others adhere to the belief that owls are shapeshifters or restless spirits of the dead. Therefore, my association with owls was marking me as a bit dark myself in certain circles. That was a great deal to absorb.

"You need to meet The Swamp Owl," Jerry advised me one day.

The Swamp Owl is a nickname for a Barred Owl, so I was confused until I learned that this Swamp Owl was a man of the Seminole Tribe. I was also surprised that he was willing to talk to me under the circumstances. I guess he had his reasons.

He wore a leather cord around his neck. Attached to it was the image of an owl carved out of alligator bone. A Swamp Owl. The Barred Owl, *Strix varia*. Swamp Owl kept a safe distance from me when we were introduced. It was a strange encounter.

I respectfully asked why he could be an owl in his tribe. What was the difference? The difference, it seemed, was in the particular owl species. His culture had no problem with the Barred Owl or several other owl species. But the one I have tattooed on my forearm, the Great Horned Owl, is quite another story, indeed.

Swamp Owl shared the reason the Horned Owl is seen as evil. Keep in mind that the following tale was verbally shared with me. There is no documentation. The traditional Native American way is to orally present the tale. I do not speak Seminole, nor do I know how to write it. But I will do the best I can to faithfully convey what Swamp Owl shared with me.

> *Long ago, in the days when our land overflowed with game and fish, lived a woman who served her tribe as a healer. She was much like a shaman to our people, offering wisdom and healing powers. The common term of the white man for our spiritual leader was medicine man or woman. Her name was Stikini.*
>
> *Stikini was hungry for power. She was greedy in her heart, thinking only of her own welfare and her knowledge of dark magic. My people began to fear her. Stories from our ancestors say that she challenged the devil himself for his throne. After a time, he struck her down but refused to serve her with death, a fate too good for her. Instead, he turned her into an immortal creature of the night, a flesh eater, a flying carnivore cursed to wander our world in search of fresh blood and flesh. She would live alone in the darkness and would be known by her people as Oopa Stikini, which was said to mean Witch Woman Owl. Crossing paths with her means death, not only to you but to your now-cursed family, too.*

Thus, Swamp Owl told me why many of the Seminole Tribe continue to uphold the beliefs and knowledge their elders have passed on to them. On that night, I was schooled.

How Can You Be a Falconer with an Owl?

"What's the difference between an owl and a hawk?
This seems to confuse many."

Falconry is the act of taking (killing) live game with a trained raptor. The original Latin meaning of *raptor* is "robber, plunderer, abductor, ravisher."[2] In English, a raptor is a bird of prey—a carnivore—and there are many different species. Keeping it simple, there are eagles, hawks, falcons, Merlins, kites, owls, hawkowls, etc. Even a vulture is a raptor but not one to hunt with. Likewise, the Bald Eagle (I'm sorry, but it just will not work).

So, one might ask, "Is a person with a hawk or an owl still a falconer if they carry the title?" The answer is yes—sort of. The truth is there are other names for falconers based on what they fly.

A person who flies a trained falcon on game animals is called a long winger. Falcons have long, stiff, pointed wings and can dive over 200 miles per hour. Flying a large broad-winged hawk like a Red-tail will label you as a game hawker. Hawks like the Red-tail are brutes with the ability to take a wide variety of mammals. Flying the smaller accipiter hawks, like a Cooper's, on the other hand, makes you an austringer. I'm told this is a German term. And hunting with a big eagle, usually a Golden or another eagle related to it, means large game can be taken, even deer. In the United States, there are only two types of eagles: the Bald Eagle and the Golden Eagle. As Bald Eagles are not used for falconry, falconers hunting with eagles are Golden Eagle falconers.

---

2   (Harper, Raptor, 2023)

Then there are a few of us that fly owls—big ones. The Eurasian Eagle Owl is such a beast. It is fearless, strong, and determined, putting it at the top of its food chain. True apex predators. Unofficially, those of us who hunt with these birds are called owlers. Personally, the title of Owl Whisperer has attached itself to me. I'm fine with it. Doing this kind of work in the public eye gets you attention that creates titles that folks can relate to: The Raptor Man, The Bird Man, The Raptor Guy, The Raptor Whisperer, The Owl Whisperer. Take your pick. We even have a nickname for our SUV truck: Gamehawker. And the one before it was Jungle Hawker. We hunted in some dense vegetation, thus the name.

The various names help children remember us and learn the meanings of the titles.

We are all falconers, either apprentice, general level, or master falconer, depending upon the training level completed.

Thorin , Eurasian Eagle Owl, inspecting a piece of property that I am purchasing.

What to Expect

"As in most generations, the youth of our world need help. They need direction to become productive citizens. Falconry can teach life skills to assist in this endeavor."

If you are reading this, I expect by now that you have some love or appreciation for raptors. Perhaps you are a birdwatcher. I am, too. Maybe a wildlife photographer? Ditto. An artist looking for a subject or a musician searching for a song? Again, I can relate. Maybe, just maybe, you think you want to become a falconer. Many try to follow this rather difficult path. And many get lost on the trail. It is not easy to do it correctly. Be prepared to follow the laws and the advice of your sponsor, spend lots of money, and worry about your birds like they are your children. In fact, they require even more long-term care than most children because while our human children usually venture out on their own at some point, your birds will require day-to-day care for the rest of their lives, which can be more than fifty years for some species.

Are you willing to give up vacations almost entirely because you cannot board a raptor? Even if you could, it would be terrible for your charge. They do not understand their bondmate disappearing for weeks, and legally, they surely cannot be left alone. Food needs to be stockpiled and kept frozen. And no, I do not mean grocery-store meat. Our raptors' diets consist of rats, mice, quail, rabbits, squirrels, and lots of day-old chickens that hatcheries routinely destroyed until we falconers figured them out. I have two deep freezers filled with this stuff, and yes it costs plenty. Thorin alone routinely eats six chickens per day, usually four of those in his morning meal.

Falconry gear is also costly, especially good gauntlet gloves. They are an art form all their own. Good ones range from $125 to $1,000. I just ordered one from Italy. It will cost $175 by the time I get it next month. The cheap ones rot in their first year.

Additionally, the mew is often a big cost. Lumber and other items can set you back $2,000 if you do all of the work yourself. Hiring a contractor adds even greater expense. There are prefab mews available, but most portables are small. You get what you pay for, right?

The mew, or mews, is a raptor house built to federal standards. In falconry circles, I've heard it said that the name comes from the fact the birds make sounds at night similar to kittens mewing. However, the term can actually be traced back to the French word meaning "to molt"—muer. [3]

---

3   (Harper, mews, 2019)

You will also need veterinary medical supplies. Consider it your very own raptor Rx station. Again … expensive but very necessary.

And most of all, raptors require your love, patience, and time—lots of time! Falconry is not a hobby. It should not be taken lightly. For example, Thorin's life expectancy is sixty to sixty-five years. Are you willing to dedicate yourself to something that will last longer than most marriages? I repeat: this is not a hobby. Jerry told me as an apprentice that if you are married and your spouse is not a falconer, having more than one bird will lead to divorce. Wow! I am permitted for five birds and currently maintaining only two. I have been married for forty-six years this spring of 2023. Luckily, Jerry wasn't right about everything.

If this sounds like I am trying to discourage you, you might just be right. Falconry takes more dedication than most can give. You cannot ignore the needs of your birds. They need you every day. They need mental stimulation and interaction. Thorin and I go out even if it's raining. In the Rockies, snow didn't stop us, either. Dr. Death, in fact, loved the snow. But the rewards? Endless.

There is no other activity in the world where an apex predator, a wild animal, a hunter like a lion, tiger, or bear, will allow a human to join their world and become an integral part of their existence. Would a great white shark allow you to tag along for a front-row seat and actually partner with you to assist in her kill? I think not.

Falconry puts you in a unique and wonderful place. There is a certain healing power offered by raptors. Humans have known it for some 5,000 years. My bonds with my birds are priceless. Maybe you, too, can experience it one day. But be ready for your life to change.

Hawks and Eagles in High Country

Back in the 1970s, Jerry was hunting pronghorn antelope out in Colorado with his Golden Eagle, Copper. They were quite a sight to behold. It would appear that a prominent passerby felt the same way as he pulled his four-by-four truck off the road and parked in the snow nearby. They were near Aspen, Colorado.

"Fa-a-a-arr out!" echoed through the valley. Jerry recognized the fellow pilot. (Did I mention Jerry flew for the Navy in his prime?)

This gentleman wore round wire-rimmed glasses, a leather cowboy hat, a denim jacket with a fluffy sheepskin liner, and a smile that stretched from ear to ear. His name was John. He asked Jerry if he could watch and then continued his education with Jerry and Copper over the next four hours or so. He said he was truly amazed by everything that unique pair had to offer. Pleasantries were exchanged, and John left, his smile never leaving his face.

Some six months later, a song was released on the radio, a local Colorado TV show, and on an album. It became popular at concerts like Red Rocks, outside Denver, Colorado. The song was titled "The Eagle and the Hawk." Imagine that. I think you can guess who John was.

I drew this as a teenager in 1975. It has followed my life everywhere!

Hibiscus Flowers and an Owl

Maintaining raptors places you square in the eyes of the government: the Fish and Game Commission, the Department of the Interior, and State and Federal Wildlife Services. Prepare to be inspected on a regular basis. My last inspection took three hours, and I passed with flying colors. It's all in a day's work.

After a time, I became fairly friendly with my inspecting officers. One asked me about some big red hibiscus flowers growing on my property. It seems he had a pet iguana that loved to eat the flowers, and he needed a supplier. "No worries!" I assured him. I had plenty. This created a situation wherein my game warden dropped by quite often. It gave him an excuse to bring new officers to my property and teach them the ropes, as it were, with my birds and my facilities.

One day, he showed up with a rookie game warden to give him the tour. We all sat down with iced tea to settle in and catch up since our last visit. The rookie was nervous, probably thinking he might be tested in some way. Well, perhaps he sort of was.

I mentioned earlier that at any time it would not be unusual to see an owl inside my house as we allowed them some freedom. This was one of those times.

Our home had a large fireplace with a thick cypress mantle that demanded visitors take a second look. Of course, there were knick-knack raptors displayed on its surface. I'm a falconer, after all. My officer friend knew that the owl, Cricket, was there. He had met her many times. He also knew that she was 100% legal. I could tell he had some plans for the rookie, who was looking more nervous by the minute.

Eventually, he asked his student if something was wrong, based on his uncomfortable body language. With hesitation, the young man began to speak. He voiced

*Screech Owl Cricket—
my living fireplace-mantle
figurine*

his concerns, saying he reviewed nothing in my records about being permitted for a taxidermy owl. He must have thought he was going to score some points as an officer. My friend chuckled softly to himself.

I clicked my tongue like you might call a horse and added a soft whistle, causing Cricket to wake up and fly to my shoulder. I thought the new officer was going to have a stroke or some other malfunction. If Cricket could have laughed, I think she would have. The rookie never returned.

Woodland Hills Birds of Prey

*"In the hills of Marion County, Woodland Hills sits
on one of the highest elevations in the area."*

It doesn't take long when living with raptors for people to start to take notice. They want to see your birds, visit your property, take photos—you name it. Various groups making these requests included schools, civic organizations and clubs, Boy Scouts, The Florida Aquarium, The Bishop Planetarium, birthday parties, picnics … well, you get the idea.

In the beginning, we did all we could and for free. It cost us dearly for a time. We were doing programs four hours away and receiving nothing to assist us with costs. We needed to get organized. So, Woodland Hills Birds of Prey was born. Since then, we have done programs for groups as large as 5,000 people, but I enjoy the smaller, more personal groups of thirty to forty. Today, we continue to be a wildlife education facility/service serving the local school system, parks, and other special venues in our surrounding community. However, our facility is no longer open to the public due to insurance restrictions. Instead, we come to you.

We were flattered once by a request to travel from Florida to Ohio for a program but politely refused due to distance and logistics. The group really wanted the original Owl Whisperer. I was pretty surprised by this but referred them to a speaker in their local region.

Media attention can also sometimes be challenging. While it is admittedly flattering to have the media support our efforts and see articles and stories about us in various newspapers and magazines, it isn't always wonderful. At times, journalists get the information wrong … with misquotes and the like. Although popularity can come with a price, I really try to take it all in stride. We have appeared on TV, too. At one time, we did commercials for WFLA-TV in Tampa, Florida. They aired four to five times a day for almost two years. People even asked for my autograph during my travels. Wow! And it is all because of the birds. People love them, and I'm just along for the ride. The birds need a solid perch.

COVID-19 really hindered our ability to work with students in the schools. We were all fully vaccinated, not to mention catching the germ ourselves a few years back. We're fine, though, and actually prefer outdoor programs anyway, but schools and teachers still often get nervous about and fear organized programs. It's really too bad. Since the start of the pandemic, all of our programs have been mostly adult in nature, visitation-wise. We use local forests and parks for these events. But it does make for a wonderful school field trip, too.

The center medallion of this design is a reverse negative of Thorin created by Jim Hepinstall, owner of Forest Hawk Falconry, producers of custom falconry equipment.

Irwin Visits Florida

We all know who Steve Irwin was. He was younger than me, but I still looked up to him as a champion of wildlife. His dedication and love for animals would take him from us in the end. I relate to him for many reasons, but in particular, I too would swim and dive with the same kind of rays. I got much closer than I should have, just like Steve, but his luck wasn't good that day. I was more fortunate and lived to write about my experiences. Oh, the stories he could have passed on.

When my mother was put in the hospital one week here in Florida due to a mini stroke, she shared her room with another very sweet lady who was extremely interested in my background with raptors. She and I spoke on many different days during my mother's recovery.

One day, she asked me if I had ever heard of Steve Irwin, The Crocodile Hunter. Of course, I had! Everyone has! Well, she told me Steve and Terri were scheduled to do a shoot in Florida about our southeastern diamondback rattlesnake. Terri is from the United States, so she personally knew people here. The Irwins are down-to-earth folks who seemed to prefer staying with friends rather than in an expensive hotel. Can you guess who they were scheduled to stay with? Yep, my mother's roommate.

I was very surprised when she invited us to stay with her that week, also, and meet Steve and Terri. *Wow!* I thought. *What an experience that could be!* I thanked her and advised her that I would address the offer with my mother privately and get back to her.

Shockingly, and rather sadly, my mother refused. She was self-conscious about being around a celebrity and felt she would not be able to relax for the entire visit. I guess I understand, but celebrity status doesn't make someone better than you, just simply on a different road in life than many others travel. Kudos to them.

My mother's refusal disappointed our new friend, but she said she understood.

However, her offer still stood firm for me. Perhaps I would meet with my wildlife hero after all. But I sensed my mother's odd disappointment. She didn't want me to go, either. (*Heavy sigh.*) So, I politely refused and watched the experience on TV.

Later, my son had the opportunity to travel to Australia, and I encouraged him to do it. I was so happy he got to experience the zoo there and everything Irwin. Cool!

My son, Ethan, Down Under at the Irwins' Australia Zoo with a nice Wedge-tailed Eagle and its handler.

And did you know that the late Steve Irwin's uncle is a raptor guy? Absolutely! Steve chased crocodiles and just about everything else, while his uncle gravitated to our birds. I always admired Steve for his energy and dedication. In fact, I was flattered and humbled on several occasions by folks referring to me as Florida's Steve Irwin. His love for wildlife was infectious. I can only hope my energy and love for the natural environment are received in the same way. Thanks, and rest in peace, Steve-O. You are missed!

Messengers of Death

*"When you somehow think that you know it all,
look at the person in the mirror and admit that you don't.
We should continue to learn until the day we die—or longer."*

I have always thought that ravens and crows were pretty awesome birds. In the wild, I use crows to locate raptors for photography purposes. They always seem to know how to find them. The flock, or murder, is a tight-knit group with a very definite leader.

We have a murder that visits our property daily. Their leader interacts with me every day. I shall call him Edgar—Edgar Allan Crow. (Yes, I'm from Baltimore; give Poe his due.) The name fit, and it stuck. He's visited for years now. I like Edgar. He impresses me.

This is Edgar Allen Crow. (It's a born-in-Baltimore thing, and I was.)

Sadly, a few years back, my bloodhound, Stella, passed away. She'd had a full life, and she passed as I kissed her one last time on her forehead. She was a large dog and needed a full grave. So, it was time to get started. As a family, my wife, my son, and I selected a location and created her resting place. I think my wife did most of the digging. And who do you suppose was watching from overhead in a pine? You guessed right: Edgar.

Stella was placed in a plastic body bag and ready to be laid to rest in her grave.

Edgar squawked one loud note, and suddenly, as if by magic, the murder arrived! Quietly, one by one, they perched overhead. I believe I counted eleven crows looking down quietly as if showing their respect to us for helping other animals. One can only imagine.

As we all paid our respects to our lost family member, the crows silently waited on. My family left me graveside with my thoughts as I heard Edgar once again utter his one-note caw. His friends departed, one after another, but he stayed. We looked at each other, that crow and I. I thanked him, and he quietly flew away.

I have also witnessed crow funerals for one of their own. It is mind-blowing.

When my Harris' Hawk, Terra, passed away a few years ago, I experienced several wildlife-related signs, and I know Jerry would have had a spiritual explanation for each. I know I, too, have become a believer after my experiences with raptors over the decades.

1. We had taken Terra to our veterinarian in her final hours. After she passed away, upon leaving the clinic, we were followed by a Bald Eagle for quite a few miles, flying directly over my truck at maybe thirty feet. It reminded me of the videos of imprinted ducks or geese following humans in a car. We lost her at highway speed.

2. I visited the town of Dunnellon, Florida, that day, too. I had nothing special in mind—just killing time in my grief. Surprisingly, a buck deer walked in front of me. He casually crossed my path as if part of a vision, but I knew that he was actually there, at a distance of only ten to twenty feet. This was within the city limits near the shopping areas. I admit that even as a forest ranger, I thought this odd. I've been close to wild deer but not in populated human areas.

3. Very similar to the deer encounter but out in the country that same day, I experienced a very large male coyote crossing a trail in front of me on planted-pine land owned by a paper company. He

was as large as a wolf, a beautiful canine indeed. He looked over his shoulder at me and moved on. It seemed like a message was delivered just to me. I will always believe it was so.

4. While all of these encounters are quite astounding in their own rights, considering the situation, the following one is the most unusual and unique. The evening of Terra's death, I set up my folding chair on a piece of my property that had been comfortable to Terra. The sun was just setting. It was time to stop and mourn. I was just settling in when I heard the distant call of a Great Horned Owl. I spotted her on the northern side of my property in the turkey oaks. I answered her in owl talk. She replied. Within minutes, I heard another Great Horned Owl call to the east. The pitch was different. This one was male, most likely mated to the big girl that I could still see. I answered him, too, and then the birds spoke to one another. Surprisingly, it did not take long until a third owl became vocal and began to communicate with me, as well. This one, another female, was on the southern end of my property. We repeated the process, and the three of them continued their beautiful calls. My experiences with Great Horned Owls have shown them to be loaners beyond their immediate family. Parents and first-year young will associate, but three appearing that day were adults. It was kind of odd. As I continued to enjoy the serenade, unbelievably, a fourth horned owl entered the songs. It was a smaller male but still an adult. This was very unusual. The feathered quartet stayed with me for half an hour or so before blending into the dark woods. I had never witnessed such a thing and doubt I ever will again. I am convinced this was for Terra … to say goodbye.

Of Wizards and Witches

"You might make a very fine wizard one day."
—from *Harry Potter and the Philosopher's Stone* by J.K. Rowling

My son was fortunate to grow up with raptors. From the time he was born, he knew them. He was handling owls by the time he was seven or eight years old. I would take him out in the field with me and fly Duster over his head. He would just laugh and smile, having the time of his life. Great memories!

Ethan living the dream—shown with baby Barred Owl Gentry

During his childhood, a story came out of the U.K. about schools of magic and owls. I even recall one character, I believe his name was Draco, having a Eurasian Eagle Owl.

We read all of the books in that series and saw the movies, too, and I often wonder, at the time, did my son just take it all in stride that everyone in the world had owls? It could have easily seemed so. But he knew about falconry and the differences that were created in the storyline of wizards.

They say that the legendary Merlin was a wizard. It is quite possible he was more real than myth. Most depictions I have seen of him seem to show him with a large owl, once again seen as a magical creature from another realm. But were Merlin and King Arthur even real, you ask? Who's to really say?

I recall a television series, *Game of Thrones*, featuring dragons along with human kingdoms fighting for power, while dangers lay in the north with the walking dead. There was a character in that program who also had a large owl. He was connected to it magically. It would fly ahead of him and their army to see what was afoot. During that time, the man went into a trancelike state and could see everything his owl could see of the enemy. It was quite a trick, and other writers have utilized it, too, in their works of fiction.

I suppose that my point is simply this: owls have been respected around the world as mystical creatures, magical even. Many people see the spiritual side of their existence. Some of the deities depicted in cave art or other record-keeping texts show them as being closely connected to owls. For centuries, we have labeled owls as being wise. We even depict them as personified scholars in books, artwork, and even TV commercials. "How many licks does it take to get to the center of a Tootsie Pop? The world may never know"—because owls cannot count. But they sure are good at many other things.

Good Things Happen
to Those Who Wait

"Find a way to relax. Maybe that special place that is only yours. Let your troubles melt away. For me, that involves being with a raptor. I go to the forest with Thorin on my arm and sit in our wild place for hours. I find it very therapeutic and relaxing. So does he."

If you are a falconer, you know it is very common for people to gravitate toward you and your bird. Yes, they will arrive at the front gate of your home. They will stop you in public. It just seems to be human nature. I take advantage of the time and steer the conversation down the educational path. After all, that's what we do with our environmental education programs. People often just do not know enough about the environment in which they live. I try to change that.

So today, some three hours ago, I was out in the state forest with Thorin, my Eurasian Eagle Owl. We were relaxing in the morning sun when we were approached by two ladies on horseback. Thorin hunkered down at the sight of the horses. I politely advised the ladies about why he seemed put off by them.

Years earlier, when I was contracted by a horse club to do a falconry presentation, I asked the attendees to not use flash photography and to keep their horses away from the birds. However, a person rode their horse right into the pavilion, anyway, where I had Thorin. The horse scared the owl so badly that to this day, if Thorin sees a horse from even fifty yards away, he will react negatively to it.

We exchanged pleasantries, and the ladies began asking questions about Thorin. One of the women asked if he was a Great Horned Owl and was surprised when I said no. I then explained his Austrian heritage. She seemed impressed with him. She then told me she had learned of falconry when she was a young girl in school and had fallen in love with the romance of the lifestyle. One thing led to another, and falconry became part of her studies and overall education. She told me she had even written college theses on falconry.

Decades later, our paths would cross on over 80,000 acres of government land. While this might not seem like much of a big deal, one other detail, in my opinion, makes it so. Before we parted, she shared with me that I was the first real flesh-and-blood falconer she had ever met. She seemed thrilled by that. I'm glad. And yes, good things do happen to those who wait: she met Master Falconer Good.

Write a Book

Earlier today, as Thorin and I were breaking in a new custom falconer's glove from Italy, I marveled at its wonderful workmanship. I often wonder why we seem to need to shop abroad for high-quality craftsmanship with things like that. At least they are available to those who search.

Later, while we were out, we attracted visitors with questions, as usual. One friendly lady spent an hour with us, talking about raptors and life. Environmental education seems to be one of the things we offer to our fellow man and woman. We are happy to serve.

Our conversation had this person laughing out loud at some of the stories I shared. When we finished our encounter, she added a personal opinion: "Mark, you need to write a book! I'd buy it in a second!"

We shall see. Thank you.

Raptors Teach English

Somewhere in this writing, it was mentioned that Jerry and I spent some time teaching teens. We worked together part-time at a drug rehabilitation center for young men. It was a residential treatment center where clients resided until becoming emotionally healthy enough to move on to better things than drugs. Jerry was their one-room schoolteacher who could reward them with a high school diploma for their efforts. I was a counselor who dealt with their personal issues and direction. We used the raptors to get through to these young men.

Jerry kept things under control with an odd form of intimidation. He brought his giant Golden Eagle, Copper, to class! Imagine youthful offenders sitting in a classroom with a monster of a raptor watching them. They had seen videos of her in action, so the reality of her presence was very apparent. Jerry used this as an introduction of sorts before really hooking them with what falconry is actually all about.

Along with being fascinated with raptors, I am also a car nut and arranged free rides in a hot-rod corvette for those who earned it. This practice was based on the theory of giving positive rewards for positive behaviors: "Work your program and win a 180-mph ride in a custom car owned by *Corvette Fever* magazine." The magazine also covered our event with an article about our efforts.

Falconry works the same way: positive rewards for positive behavior. Never negatively respond to a raptor, and be very careful to consider other options before using negative reinforcement with other animals or even kids, too.

I was also an instructor at a Florida Forest Service-owned facility for teen male offenders. I taught forestry-related classes, fire behavior, weather, chain of command, and similar subjects. I also substituted for History and English. The latter was my favorite of the two, for my purposes.

After a bit of effort with the school board, I was given permission to utilize my raptors officially to teach those students. Much like Jerry, I started bringing raptors to school.

Certain students, selected based on their interests and grades, were introduced to two of my birds that would be our subjects for the class. I wasn't trying to make them into falconers, but they needed to learn how to hold a hawk and owl properly. While learning these basics, they became comfortable with my birds. The Barred Owl for the class was Gentry, and the Harris' Hawk was Terra.

Meanwhile, I gave the students assignments to research the background of the raptors. It started like a book report to keep it simple. Little did they know of my secret plans to really challenge them.

Preparation took an entire term. No kidding. Then I took them to the next level.

"Gentlemen, it's time for your assignments." They looked at me, perplexed. "Your research is going to be turned into a public-speaking assignment with live birds." I still remember the fear on their faces.

We had three more weeks until a scheduled public appearance about raptors. Each student would present their research to a class of elementary school students while holding their live subject. They were scared, to say the least.

The common fear for my students was not knowing the correct information to respond with should one of the elementary students question them. I reassured them that I would never leave them hanging if they faltered but to remember something: "To those younger children, you are an adult at age eighteen. Holding the birds, you are the experts. Be confident."

And so, they were.

We spoke to approximately 150 kids that day, and it was perfect in every way. The confidence level of those young men just skyrocketed into another realm.

Raptors can heal the hurting. They can help you focus and aid in your understanding of life and the world around you. And they can teach in ways you might never imagine. They still teach me every day.

And yes, English credits were given to my students towards their high school diplomas. Pretty nice!

Forestry and Falcons

"Dedicated to her Memory"

Generally speaking, working as a wildland firefighter offers opportunities to engage with wild animals at relatively close range. Sooner or later, you see everything. It keeps the job interesting. Depending on what state you live in, the variety of wildlife can be astounding. In Florida, of course, it's the alligators in every watering hole and the venomous snakes.

In the Rocky Mountains, the Grizzly Bear got my attention on several excursions. Every part of the country seems to have something that will get your attention. I always look for raptors. Imagine that.

Remember the travel games you would play with your family on road trips? Maybe you did the "Punch Buggy" game. Or maybe you counted various license plates on cars. Could you locate fifty states? It was a fun way to pass the time.

My favorite was always "Raptor Identification." With this game, not only do you need to spot them from a moving car, but you also need to identify them in the blink of an eye.

I look for raptors everywhere. Under most circumstances, the results are good. But at times, not so much. Forest fires—and sadly, prescribed fires—cause much harm.

As a raptor lover and a falconer, I was always on the lookout for issues in scenarios regarding fire and animals. In the southeastern United States, nesting season for raptors is in February and March. Prescribed fire should be avoided during these times. Vultures, which are also raptors, nest on the ground. Fire will certainly destroy their nests and eggs, or babies if they have hatched, and the parents will die trying to save them. Raptors make dedicated parents and take extreme measures to save their young.

While I have witnessed far too many raptor deaths in my lifetime, there are a few that stay in my heart.

One such occurrence was a family of Barred Owls. Someone put up a nest box years ago on forestry-service property. I believe it was a biologist. Years passed and the box began to fall apart. These boxes need to be replaced because owls are creatures of habit and will return annually without understanding the box is no longer safe. Someone on staff dropped the ball.

Owls moved in and hatched one baby. It was in February. To make things worse, the forestry service set fire in the immediate area. The bottom of the box was 50% gone due to rot.

Well, the bottom fell out and the owlet fell to the forest floor. The parents were stressed beyond belief trying to help their young offspring. I attempted a rescue, but the flames and smoke were just too much, and the owlet died. A piece of me died that day, too. I hate the senseless loss of life that could have been prevented. If you see boxes and such on government lands, please report the damages to the authorities. You just might save a life.

The second incident that sticks in my mind is one of a falcon protecting her nest. My partner and I were patrolling a fire line when we noticed a frantic bird flying around a snag, a dead tree. The smoke was very thick, but I could tell the bird was a falcon. For a prescribed fire, that tree should have been prepped, which requires hand-stripping bark from the tree, raking the base to remove fuels that could torch the tree, and then burning a fifty-foot circle around the tree to prevent ignition. This is also done to protect woodpecker nesting trees. But because it is extremely time consuming, many teams ignore this work.

We helplessly watched the mother falcon trying to rescue her young trapped in the nest inside the dead tree. We knew that her chances were slim and the nest contents were already destroyed.

We watched her give in to the elements and crash near the base of the tree. I couldn't help myself and went into rescue mode, running through the flames to save the raptor. She was still breathing when I located her but very much in shock. My partner called in our situation with our dispatch, asking permission to rush the bird to a local veterinarian some thirty minutes away. His request was refused. We next took a chance and planned to ignore our orders and take the falcon to the vet anyway.

Sadly, we failed. Within five miles, she passed away in my arms. This was another tragic loss that could have been avoided. I mourn for every one of these beautiful creatures.

Preventable loss of life has no valid excuse. This applies to all life, not just raptors.

We buried her near her tree after it was safe to return. The male was never seen.

*Assisting with an injured Barred Owl
at Nature World Wildlife Rescue Sanctuary, Inc.*

Assisting at a Rehabilitation Facility

When I first became interested in raptors, a friend of mine suggested that I could learn more volunteering at a wildlife rehabilitation center. So, I decided to do just that.

During the first day at the center, they received a large brown raptor. I honestly thought it was a young eagle. Foolish mortal. I had much to learn as I stood there admiring a beautiful juvenile female Red-tailed Hawk. I still laugh at myself when I look back on these memories. Ya gotta start somewhere.

This prompted me to learn more—as much as I could. It was time to learn. So, I did.

While handling a bird in a medical environment, you are forced to do things you want to avoid with your falconry charge, restraint being one example. Raptors do not forget, and medically handled birds usually develop a fear of man, making it impossible to bond with them, for the most part. Remember my advice about doing nothing negative to your bird. They simply do not forget.

If you raise a young bird, teach it to be touched and handled. Make it comfortable with an exam so if they really need it, they won't freak out. Training and trust: they work. In my opinion, every falconer should spend a year volunteering at a good wildlife center so they can learn about identification, handling techniques, medical procedures, medication dosages, disease identification, and related issues. They will use every bit of this knowledge with their own birds.

Learn all you can through volunteering, then enter your training as an apprentice falconer. You will come to treasure your time at the wildlife facility, and your experiences there also might just help you save your bird's life one day. God bless our rehabbers.

My Organic Kite

"I'll bet you have never done this!"

Throughout these chapters, I have mentioned wildlife rehabilitators and what they do for animals many times. They can play a vital role in teaching upcoming falconers how to handle many medical issues with their birds. Especially during the apprentice phase of training, students of falconry simply cannot afford veterinary care for their charges. You learn to handle most issues on your own. It's a learning process.

While working with Jerry as his assistant director of the Masters of the Wind program at Cypress Gardens, we assisted rehabbers from all over the State of Florida. I believe they felt, at times, that a falconer's touch was a way to help a raptor on the road to recovery. Maybe so. There is also a certain amount of individual creativity or a fresh perspective with a falconer in situations that are out of the ordinary.

Enter Seminole Wind, a Bald Eagle. Seminole came to us at the facility as an adult eagle. His head and tail were white, which confirmed to us that he was a mature bird. Bald Eagles are almost solid brown until their fifth or sixth year of maturity, and some are streaked with brown in their white areas until fully mature.

Seminole had a wing/shoulder injury, so he could not fly when he arrived. The rehabber who provided Seminole to us had no way to test Seminole's progress. They had hoped we could make him whole once again. We knew we would try all of our tricks of the trade to make that happen.

We started with basic jumps to the glove for food, which initially took time with the wild eagle. Some say that a rule of thumb for getting a raptor to do that basic step is sixty hours on average. Then there are birds like my Shiloh that just step right up like they were born to it. Seminole was not one of those.

Once he learned the glove hop, we gradually extended our distance from him when calling him to the glove. This is how it is done, usually within a structure like a mew if large enough. Eventually, in order to extend the distances, we needed to move outside in the open. The next step was done with a line attached to prevent escape and possible harm. It is a strong but light nylon line called a creance line that can be altered in length as needed. Care must be exercised to prevent any entanglement in trees, bushes, and powerlines, and a large area is necessary.

Over a period of weeks, we used this kind of exercise to strengthen the area of Seminole's injury.

Seminole grew stronger day by day. I did notice that he held his wing at an odd angle from the shoulder, though, which limited his full flight capabilities. As we continued his training, I felt that emotionally, this interaction was positive, and if he was determined to be non-releasable, the training would prepare him for a new life as a wildlife ambassador, teaching old and young alike.

It was time to become creative.

We were already flying Seminole distances of up to 100 feet, and he would attempt altitude on occasion. I would slowly and gently bring him down as he tired.

"Extend the line," Jerry directed. "We need to be sure."

And so, I did. Seminole was fitted with a 500-foot creance line with the hope that he could indeed gain altitude and fly like the eagle he was meant to be.

We had lift-off!

It took him some effort, but he managed to extend the entire 500 feet of line. I was flying a living Bald Eagle like a kite! Good lord, what an experience! Jerry was grinning from ear to ear and laughing out loud. Admittedly, it was a very emotional experience. To this day, even now as I write, I shed a tear or two thinking about Seminole and his ordeal and progress.

While I'd like to end his story with a successful release to the wild, I cannot. His final flights in training continued to show that he struggled with full extension of the wing. Could he hunt? Would he become hunted? Jerry and I spent much time pondering this subject.

In the end, Seminole could not be released because we feared it would cause an early death for him.

Ambassador, then, it was!

Seminole was renamed and transferred to a wildlife education facility like our own. His training with us made him the perfect bird for this purpose. He was treated like a king and met thousands of people to whom this story could be shared.

Blow, blow, Seminole Wind. Bless you! (I miss my "organic kite.")

Injuries Inflicted
by Your Own Charge

"So, you plan to adopt or legally capture a raptor.
Expect some adjustment in how your bird reacts to you.
'Fight or flight' is a common expression. How would you feel if your
beautiful baby attacked your face? Food for thought."

In this chapter, I am not trying to make you fear raptors but instead to respect them as the predators they are. Working with them pretty much guarantees that incidents will happen that make you bleed. Yes, even if accidental, injuries will happen.

Thorin has never acted or reacted aggressively toward me. However, his feet are large and his talons are long. He has a tendency to step off of the glove with one foot and stand on my bare forearm near the elbow. Yes, those stiletto toes cut my arm each time, and I bleed weekly. Sometimes, it doesn't even hurt because the talons are so sharp.

Never try to handle a raptor without a glove!! I see untrained handlers attempting this, and it is foolishness. Allowing an owl to sit on your head is also risky. With almost two-inch-long talons on a Great Horned Owl and a reported ability to squeeze at 450 psi in each foot, your brain is very close to serious injury. Even a simple loss of balance could have those talons in your eyes!

Years ago, during a medical exam at our local vet, it happened to me with my dear Great Horned Owl, Shiloh, still my baby girl now at age thirty-four. The exam was simple enough. Routine. I was advised that due to insurance restrictions, I would not be allowed to hold Shiloh for the exam. The vet tech was very young, with limited raptor experience, if any. I stayed close.

Well, things went south quickly when Shiloh started to struggle, and the girl released her hold in fear of being grabbed. To protect her and restrain Shiloh, I was forced to cover that exploding hand grenade with my chest as I attempted to grab the bird's ankles. While I succeeded in protecting everyone there but myself, Shiloh's talons found their mark.

She managed to grab my throat and chin badly, causing blood to go everywhere. I honestly thought she had cut my jugular vein. My white shirt was crimson red in just minutes. She had attacked out of fear, which had triggered her fight-or-flight response. Raptors are good fighters. Shiloh had no idea she had hurt me, but it comes with the territory. To this day, I wear a goatee.

My Harris' Hawk, Terra, was a "squeezer." She loved to bear down on my glove until her talons pierced the three layers of leather! Yes, they penetrated my arm, too. Blood would fill my glove while I waited for her to release her quarry. With a bird on your arm, the glove stays. Injuries can be extreme, and you can't even see them right away. In regard to Terra, the answer was a Kevlar glove, made of the same material as a bulletproof vest. It worked perfectly!

In falconry, you will get hurt—sooner or later.

My beautiful Barred Owl, Gentry, had his own issues based on fear. He'd had a rough initial upbringing when the school kids almost killed him. While I believed we had a good relationship, at times his fears caused aggression. In his twenty-two years with us, I can recall at least six injuries he inflicted on me.

Our worst situation was pretty simple. I visited him in his mew one day as he rested on a perch. When I approached him, he was staring at my eyes. I know now that he was seeing his own reflection in my eyes and thought it was another owl.

Suddenly, he attacked. One foot, with all four talons, took hold of my nose. The other foot grabbed my eye. Two talons actually penetrated my eyelid and pierced behind my eye. The other two on that foot went under my eye to the socket. Had he not released, I would have had my eyeball removed by a raptor!

The nose injury caused nerve damage that lasted for years. My eye turned black and blue as it became more swollen every day for a week. As a first responder, I treated myself medically and packed my eye with antibiotics. It was pretty intense.

Did he do anything wrong? Not really. Jerry would say that Gentry was just being an owl. Admittedly, for a while, I used extra caution with him, but we got past it and stayed friends.

But this stuff happens. Expect it. The longer you work with raptors, you'll find you will get hurt. It simply comes with the territory. Falconers learn to live with these injuries.

Once again, is falconry for you? Only you know for certain. It isn't for everyone—that's for sure!

It Happened Yet Again

"Might I have your autograph, please?"

On March 24, 2023, during another day in the forest with my Eurasian Eagle Owl, Thorin, we were once again approached by people on horses as they rode off into a Wildlife Management Area (hunting area), seemingly without a care in the world. Warning signs were posted, yet they wore no orange colors to increase their visibility, and you could clearly hear guns being fired within a half mile of our location.

They saw Thorin and came in our direction. I politely requested they not approach with the horses and explained Thorin's distaste for them. I then allowed a photo session after the horses were moved away.

During this time, I was shocked at their lack of concern regarding the possibility of getting shot. Years ago, I lost a friend to a hunting accident. He was shot from behind by a hunter and died in the field. I take this subject very seriously. Sadly, some do not.

Shortly after speaking with the two women, a game warden arrived. She was new to me and after a few introductions, advised me she was fairly new to the job, too. She was excited to meet Thorin and even got to watch him eat a snack, his fourth chicken chick of the morning. We were not hunting that day, so I carried a food supply for him. It was, however, turkey season on government lands.

Our new officer asked many questions about us and Woodland Hills Birds of Prey. Thorin's background connected to smuggling intrigued her as stopping this type of crime, she told us, is dear to her heart. I wish her well.

After looking at my permits and my book, which consists of thirty-five years of letters of appreciation for our efforts over the decades, she said she had spent some military time in the Middle East and had been introduced to falconry there. She sported several raptor-related tattoos and admired my own depicting my Great Horned Owl, Shiloh.

I was taken aback when she sheepishly commented that talking to me made her feel like she was in the presence of a celebrity. I blushed. She is a kind soul.

What she did next surprised me. In my truck, I carry copies of some publications that have featured us. When I gave her one, she asked for my autograph—no kidding—and she had me date it. This was the first autograph I had been asked to sign in a very long time.

Thank you, Officer Conner! You made my day!

We save all of the dropped feathers from each of our birds!
When possible we have donated to Native American facilities
in Florida.

To Sum Things Up

"Having an apex predator—in this case, a raptor—preen your eyebrows is one thing. Allowing them to preen your eyelids and eyelashes is quite another. Trust."

Falconry is not for everyone. It is an extremely time-consuming activity that quite honestly becomes a lifestyle very quickly. It can be overwhelming yet more rewarding than almost anything I can think of. Falconry, raptors, and all of the connecting elements have directed my lifestyle to places I never imagined and offered me the ability to meet and befriend people worldwide. It has introduced me to so many birds and all of those unique personalities that came with each and every one.

Starting as an apprentice falconer as a younger person offers character-building challenges that otherwise may never be learned by a teen in today's society. If you start a bit later in life, no matter. Just remember to holster any opinions you may have developed earlier in life as a non-falconer. Some folks have trouble doing that and wearing the trainee mantle. One needs to open both heart and mind when entering this new and exciting world. And ultimately, there is no end to the learning process because your falconry experience should continue to grow and expand with your desires and abilities.

They say that basic animal care, like caring for a dog or cat, will actually lengthen a person's life because they are dedicated to caring for another. I see it. My dog is vitally important to me and definitely helps me to relax and enjoy the more basic aspects of my life. And with luck, a large dog might live into their lower teens. But as I previously mentioned, the Eurasian Eagle Owl can exceed sixty years in its lifetime! The task of caring for one is not to be taken on by the faint of heart. Only you know for sure if this appeals to you. Remember to do what is best for your bird(s), not for yourself. You will find that this act will ultimately become what is best for you, too. Funny how it works out that way.

As humans, we all search for ourselves and what makes us special or unique. We were put on this earth for a reason, each and every one of us. I didn't really find this myself until I was in my third decade on this planet. When I finally located this lifestyle, I was somehow reborn with new knowledge and a dedication to share that with others. It is quite rewarding for me.

If you are reading this but feel falconry is out of your reach for personal reasons, don't fret. You can follow falconry through the old-school method of reading books. You can also follow falconers on social media. But use caution; like anything else, there are some who may not represent the sport as well as others. Feel free to judge as you like. Falconry demonstrations are available, too, but do some research to be sure you will be seeing a real, practicing falconer, not someone just flying birds around for a piece of meat (which is not falconry). Find movies where falconry is addressed. Even surrounding yourself with depictions of raptors and falconry can keep you in the center of things. For example, particular home décor items can add to this immersion.

Over the years, Jerry repeatedly told me that falconry is really all quite simple in the grand scheme of things: "Falconry is the sport or art of taking live game with a trained raptor. Anything else simply is not falconry." That is worth some serious thought, as I have watched people over the decades doing everything but exactly that.

Thank you for caring and absorbing my words and thoughts. I was truly born in the summer of my twenty-eighth year! Godspeed.

"Turn off the phone. You need not be connected to anyone 24/7.
Your phone will hold your messages. Smartphones are still new,
and we personally did just fine without them.
Learn to relax again. Callers will call you at another time."

Acknowledgments

A very special thank you to my late friend and falconry sponsor, Jerry Hollifield. We spent years together traveling the United States in search of raptors and new hunting areas wherever we went.

Thank you to Mary Opall, the owner of Nature World Wildlife Rescue Sanctuary, Inc., of Crystal River, Florida. She is a world of information and always helpful, no matter the challenge.

Special kudos to Juanice Christian for putting up with me while I bounced ideas off of her as she typed the roughly 17,000 words that document my activities and memories. Thank you.

And finally, thank you to all of the raptors that came and went in my life. After all, without them, there would be no wonderful stories to share.

References

American Ornithological Society. (2023). *Checklist of North and Middle American Birds.* Retrieved from American Ornithological Society: https://checklist.americanornithology.org/taxa?search=Harris%27s+Hawk

Harper, D. (2019, January 08). *mews.* Retrieved from Online Etymology Dictionary: https://www.etymonline.com/word/mews

Harper, D. (2023). Raptor. Retrieved from Online Etymology Dictionary: https://www.etymonline.com/word/raptor

About the Author

Mark Joseph Good was born in Baltimore, Maryland, but left his home state at the age of nineteen. Between Florida and Colorado, Mark served over forty years in forest management and forest wildland firefighting. Throughout his career, Mark has received many distinguished awards:

- The Governor's Distinguished Service Award under two Florida governors: Lawton Chiles and Jeb Bush
- The Department of Agriculture Outstanding Service Award presented by Commissioner of Agriculture Bob Crawford
- The Florida Park Service Heroism Award for saving lives during river flooding during a storm
- The Award of Valor presented by National Park Service Director Fran Manella for saving drowning boaters in an alligator-infested river at night
- The Interpreter of the Year (public speaker) for the Department of Environmental Protection within the Park Service of Florida

These forms of recognition are but some of many over the years.

Praise for the Author
and
Woodland Hills Birds of Prey

"Mr. Good's depth of knowledge and experience in this area is most awe-inspiring. Through his eloquent delivery, Mr. Good enlightened all of us not just to facts and figures regarding this little-understood aspect of nature, but rather educated us to understand the ways in which birds of prey impact our lives as humans."

— Howard A. Kerner
Professor, English and Communications
Winter Haven, Florida

"What an outstanding experience!"

— Jean Hehn
Middle School Teacher
Plant City, Florida

"I don't believe I've ever seen that many students listen so attentively for that length of time!"

— Gini Blair
Elementary School Teacher
Lakeland, Florida

"We've traveled in all 48 continental states and the Canadian provinces, and his programs are the most informative, interesting, and well-presented of any we have attended in State, National, or Provincial Parks."

— Dorothy and Arthur Linton
Retired
Seminole, Florida

"We were extremely impressed by your fascinating program about Birds of Prey!"
— Ivy Kelly
The Florida Aquarium
Instructor, Learning Lab
Tampa, Florida

"I appreciate knowing of your support for increased protection for wild and exotic birds. I share your view that we must be fervent in our efforts to promote the humane treatment of all wildlife, be it at home or anywhere in the world."
— Bob Graham
United States Senator

"Speaking for all four kindergarten teachers, I can honestly say that your ability to interact with the kids on their level is outstanding!"
— Janet B. Robbins
Kindergarten Teacher
Lakeland, Florida

"I don't know anyone more dedicated to saving the environment in this state than that man ..."
— Bob Hite
News Anchorman
WFLA-TV, Channel 8, Tampa, Florida

For more information about Woodland Hills Birds of Prey,
Home of Thorin Oakenshield,
follow us on Facebook
or call 352-489-9362.